Flowers, only if they're from you

Zellia Enjoli Tatiana

Copyright © 2022 Zellia Enjoli Tatiana

All rights reserved. No part of this book may be reproduced in any form or by any means, electronic or mechanical, including photo-copying, recording, or by any information storage and retrieval system, without written permission from the author. This excludes a reviewer who may quote brief passages in a review.

Cover Design: Zellia Enjoli Tatiana

Published by G Publishing LLC

Library of Congress Control Number: 2022911544

ISBN: 978-0-9985990-0-7

Printed in the United States of America

All of us

world changers,

creators,

artists…

think of our parents.

Even if just ordinary people,

we may have become

their greatest dreams

come true.

or their donation to

a more beautiful humanity,

just by having been created.

thank you for daring

to be your

full self.

That's exactly what I'm doing.

For love.

And all the ways

It has made me over.

Flowers, only if they're from you

Zellia Enjoli Tatiana

You love me with a love that's amazed by every little thing I do.

Abstract or in touch.

In color or greyscale.

Front ways or backwards, you always swoop around and love me.

You wrap me up in your love 'til I drown. You help me edit my truest versions of self.

Imperfect or improving.

Practically or in theory.

Both now and later, you always find the pathway to love me.

They say offer them up while we are still living.

Flowers, they say, give them now.

Never something I would request or demand,

and I can honestly say I am not a huge fan...

and I will take flowers,

only if they're from you.

Index

Flowers, only if they're from you

Blossom

My Favorite

No one sweeter than you

Filter Chaos

A million moments with you…

To Protect the Castle

Feelings I wish I could bottle up

Tell Me What You Need

Symphony

Weather Report

Crazy ~~In Love~~

Reach For Me

The morning of/The morning after

More Than

A Birthday Wish for Self

Sister Love

Re-Bloom

Wildflower

Stand Up in Love

Together

City Girl

We be sun people

Darkness

The Question

Shout at God

Black is an elixir

Crying Black (rap song)

"Holier than thou"

"First African American to…"

Civil Rights Act of 2020

What Being American means

Petals

Forget-Me-Nots

Untitled (Airport Love)

Disparate Elements

Good Grief (a failed relationship monologue)

Up in Arms

Karma

Better Off

If I Needed You

Broken One

Dramamine

Seeds

A Note on Love #1,462

The smell of you

Feels So Right

Place Your Hands

Borders

And you can't get full swallowing lies

Confused Heart

And so, you'll never get a taste

Thermal

Like a script

Philodendron

Nowadays

The Plague

Quarantine

The sympathy section… (quasi-photo collage)

Pandemic

Georgia Rain

P&DC

Racism is not a feeling

NOW

Sick

Running out of it

If Only… (a poem for Wilson Ali Calvin; January 30, 1993 – December 25, 2021)

Losing You

I've lived my life for so many other people

Blossom

My Favorite

she lets me

draw on my clothes.

because they are just clothes.

she lets me stay up,

and stay out late;

because she says that's what my youthfulness wants from me.

she reminds me of why

I have collections;

and why I am the way I am.

she makes me

celebrate my successes

and names them all eminent.

she sees me

stretch out

in my moments of darkness

and she directs me

back toward where she sees the light breaking through.

back toward my light.

she learns

new things about me

and vows to

never forget.

writes them down even.

she can find the art in everything.

like how chemists say

"it's all around us".

use any writing utensil or material

to color.

use any surface as canvas enough

to draw and paint.

sit still long enough and she will sketch you.

my favorite artist turned me into one too.

No one sweeter than you

I compare the way you love me

to no other feeling

I have known.

giving grace, I never earned.

extending mercy, I don't deserve.

becoming so flexible,

no matter the obstacle,

to do for me.

I can sing about how

you are like honey,

as you love me.

I can cry about who

I might be

without you and all your sweetness.

No one's love for me

has ever

felt stronger.

Not

one

love

tastes sweeter than yours.

No one

I have

ever known

is sweeter than you.

Filter Chaos

As I search for peace inside myself, I think of you. How you manage to keep breathing, like you've got a filter for the chaos in the wind around you.

A million moments with you…

only leaves me

wanting

ten million more.

To Protect the Castle

I'd rather

build a moat

around us

than to share

our palace…

our kingdom of a love

with anyone else.

such castles do not exist,

impenetrable ones.

and then there's us.

brick,

laced to kiss a spread of cement,

each time we touch

it's like I'm frozen

into and onto you.

no need to gather the tinder

for the fire—

our love.

it will never,

ever

go out.

such flames do not exist,

inextinguishable ones.

and then there's us.

I'd rather

cast an army

to do away with any challenges

than to think

of fighting

for your heart

on the battlefield of love.

though I know

such hearts do not exist.

indestructible ones. like ours.

Feelings I wish I could bottle up

but not for sale.

Just for me.

My mom's hot food on fine china; the way my heart swells and beats gladly as we say grace.

how I'd always cry on the first day of school. through grade school. even in college. that anxiousness. that fire in me to ace the courses. that same kid in me, crying, wishing my mom could be my paraprofessional.

my every, first kiss. or best kiss. or all those. in separate jars, of course. or my best orgasms too.

after a good, long conversation with a good friend. that feeling.

our embrace, after I haven't seen my woman in a while.

being cold then wrapping up in a heated blanket. the way my bones start to hum.

remembering love through a lens of laughter. those knee-slappers, tear-jerkers, leave-on-repeat type jokes; simply for the joy.

Tell Me What You Need

Tell me what you need.

Hoping that it's sweet.

Enough to follow me into the next room.

The next day.

The next eve.

Tell me what you need.

Let it be most complete.

Thorough—top to bottom of the sheet.

(With) no lines,

a blank canvas just for your release.

Tell me.

Whether it be physical

or of the meta—

I want peace for you always.

Tell me what you need.

I'll fold the corners of the pages that hold parts you love re-reading.

I'll warm your leftovers in the oven.

I'll crank my patience into overdrive.

I'll laugh when you laugh and

cry when you cry.

And we can tend the garden, together, on our knees.

Tell me what you need.

Hoping that it's me.

My heart is open to you, full disclosure…

(So) need me.

into the next room.

the next day.

into the next eve.

Love on you

how you want to be

loved on…

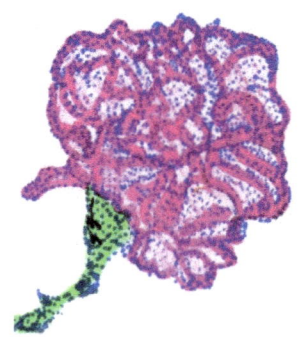

Symphony

I don't know how many songs

we have written

with our bodies,

together,

in this bed.

And with our sounds,

floating in the air

above our heads,

wherever we go.

Too many songs,

probably.

Way too many,

for me to have

kept a good count of our discography.

Weather Report

There's a storm coming in.

And you know what that means.

I will dodge no wetness.

I will wear no poncho.

I will turn my umbrella upside down

and run to you.

We will run inside and crack the window…

Crack the window

and climb in

and cuddle up close.

Make it known,

my body is on

full forecast.

Rolling thunder

and never-ending rain.

Please cause a surge and change the forecast.

Crazy ~~In Love~~

All you

have to do

is give me that look

and it's on.

Zippers down

and panties thrown.

So, you wanna

kiss me everywhere?

Swallow me whole.

Kisses…

Neck. Nipples. Navel.

Consuming my collar bone.

Wrapped around my feet and toes.

Etch your love

on my skin,

like I'm made of stone.

Then crown me.

And once on my throne,

I will look you

in your eyes

and call you crazy.

Reach For Me

like I'm the cereal

on top of the refrigerator.

even before

bowl and spoon.

ready for the taste,

at the top of the morning.

Reach for me.

like I'm the car keys

on the kitchen table.

with intention

and anticipation,

with caution

and glee.

trusting I can take you

near or far.

Reach for me

like herbal tea

and organic honey…

like salve

and shea butter.

Knowing that my love

is the healing factor.

Reach for me.

like I'm

the edge of the cover

and the room

just got a bit drafty.

pull me over

your right shoulder

and drift off

as my warmth

settles over you.

The morning of

I thought you were my soul mate.

I knew it was you,

from across the

parking lot.

Your aura

sent light rays

straight to me.

The morning after

She is

frying fish.

with no clothes on.

Got her robe wide open…

and she

must be too.

Grits and pancakes.

I knew she was my soulmate.

More Than

I almost wish it *was*

about sex

when it comes to *you*.

But

instead,

it's about

everything.

It's about

all

the

things.

More **than love.**

And more **than sex.**

It's beyond **sex,**

the concerns in my soul about you.

A Birthday Wish for Self

May you take a moment to reflect on all your accomplishments, blessings and continued fervor.

Take a moment to forgive yourself for your mistakes.

Take a moment to rest. For more than just a night or two days at a time.

Might you take a moment to reimagine the sectors that might feel out of place? Reimagine them. Please take a moment to.

Remember how much you love being alive by doing and eating your favorite things, going and being in your favorite places or maybe by taking up more space.

Receive love. It will warm and heal you.

Remember how far you've come. The low vibrations you rode on like they were normal because you had to.

Leave the past only to learn from because it's unreachable in every other capacity. Leave it only to be cherished.

Believe that you will reach new heights, even when you feel scared or fearful. Remember that "action is the anecdote to fear".

Take a moment to name your desires and intentions with specificity. Then take some time to steady yourself as you simply get ready to receive.

Oh, and Happy Birthday, Self! I wish you many more!

Sister Love

I'd be so lost without you, sister
I've always had your love to hold me up

I'd be so cold without you, sister
I've always had your love to warm me up

I'd be so sad without you, sister
I've always had your love to make me laugh

I'd be so mean without you, sister
I've always had your love to soothe me

I'd be so weak without you, sister
I've always had your love for muscles

I'd be so afraid without you, sister

I've always had your love as my protection

I'd be so penniless without you, sister

I've always had your love as wealth and needs met

I'd be so naïve without you, sister

I've always had your love to steer me righteously

I'd be so bored without you, sister

I've always had your love to light the pathway to fun

I'd be so incomplete without you, sister

I've always had your love as part of me

Re-Bloom

WildFlower

never to be tamed

or snapped at her stem.

never to grow

on schedule,

with the rest of them.

never to know

a life

without sun and pouring rain.

planting roots,

in backyard bends,

and next to tracks for trains.

never to be picked or plucked

just because.

safe from all the

made-up-world,

the wildflower was…

Stand Up in Love

stand up in love

and feel vindicated.

pound for pound,

round for round,

mad syndicated.

I'm tellin' you

I need love

and that I deserve it.

I'm tellin' you

I be love.

I cook it and serve it.

Anyone that won't

feed love

doin' me a disservice.

Anyone that's a

real one

then they're lovin' you

on purpose.

Tell you you're worth it.

Bend over backwards,

jump the cliff.

Cause no hurt s***.

Sit on your lap,

light the spliff.

Clean up your

dirt, quick.

Clear the box

of previous cats.

Queen of this turf here,

no need to

double check or ask.

You can step forward,

then back and

fall into place.

Where love is light

and light is grace.

And grace

mixed with some

mercy

got us this far.

Can't be fearful

of the haters,

if a lover's

what you are.

Wanna stand up

in love

and feel vindicated.

Pound for pound,

round for round,

mad syndicated.

A coach of anything

don't gotta ask

if I'm dedicated.

We can grow it.

Love.

Wage it.

Cultivate it.

Together

we were

made

to be together.

all of us.

we were never meant

to be all alone.

so if I tell you

that I'm lonely,

I hope you'll come…

City Girl

Once

I went shopping

in New York.

shopping for a better future.

I left

with empty plans

and a heart that knew better.

a heart that knew New York was nothing like my city.

I still wanted Detroit.

I wanted the grey skies

and the sounds of screeching brakes on city buses.

I wanted

how its allurement has its seasons.

I wanted how its blight looked back at me and mattered.

I missed my city.

All the familiar

street signs and shortcuts.

All the bows and breaks

of my neighborhood.

All the folks who bought its

first homes and shops and diners.

All the makeovers

and grand vacancies.

fights and flights and protests, in black and white photographs.

progress, in color.

All the silly of me to think New York could catch my eye. or win my heart.

I have always wanted Detroit.

And in that way

I know

I will always be a

City Girl.

We be sun people

and so they come to us for Light.

We be sun people,

and they bathe in us when in our shadow.

We be sun people;

earth melted and molded clay.

We be sun people,

and they stay

chasing us down

for the view.

We be sun people.

and too bright

to photograph

or trap in space

or time.

We be *Sun*…

Darkness

Naw.

I haven't read the transcripts.

Don't tell me you did.

...

No tellin' if the man's family

has slept.

'Cause you p i g s

will always

lose

this.

sword **fight.**

word **fight.**

who is right fight.

or any other against our Blackness.

Naw.

I don't need a video

to know that

y'all shootin' into what ya'll think is darkness.

No hesitation.

… to know

this is Blackness

y'all shootin' down.

This is life.

You cockin' back at. Pointin' at. Pumpin' lead full of.

This ain't no plain darkness ya'll shootin' into.

The Question

is not if racism is still alive.

It is.

The question is not

if racism is real.

It is.

The question is

"Can you see it?"

The question is,

"Do you see it?"

That is the beginning of discourse.

Shout at God

Ask why and for how long it's gonna hurt this way.

God… The only who thoroughly knows how deep our wells go.

Shout… In combination with your crying; try to let some of the anger pass through you. You try to. To let some of the unknowns pass through you.

To calm your heart. "Calm my heart, this instant!"

You beg, when you shout.

Shout at God…

Black is an elixir

… and they **have**
found magic
in our blood before now.
they **want a way**
to package and store
Black, somehow.
short tales of them
using our blood to buy youth.
finder's fee bypassed
for every time
they **stole a tooth.**

Black is an elixir.

<small>They</small> would drink Black down,

if it were potion.

Perfect skin we are in.

<small>They</small> would rub it all over,

if Black were lotion.

short tales of

filling furniture

with Black hair for cushion.

Pulled the country up ourselves,

if left to <small>them</small>

we'd still be pushin'.

Took our patents

and inventions,

from our hands and our brains.

A new lifetime

will begin before

we are free from

segregation's stains.

Black is an elixir. **There is no denying; the amount of real magic to** them **we've been supplying.**

in spite of their **lies and deceit,** their **pride and selfish greed; crosses burning in front yards and racist riots on the streets.**

in spite of their **set ups and systems of inequity. how we fight to stay afloat in a pool of stereotypes, even in our youth.**

an elixir…

in spite of every rape and murder scene that's never made the computer, tv or phone screen and never will. the harassment, the maltreatment, the horror stories that do not make the news.

in spite of being the strongest and smartest.

in spite of our way with rhythm being commercialized, our cuisine being frozen and mass manufactured, our style of dress being copied and sold. our beauty, mimicked.

in spite of our setbacks being nothing more than leaves in the wind to them…

In spite of being unarmed, we are always shot dead on sight.

Black is that elixir—

mad they **cannot keep their grip on us tight.**

Crying Black (rap song)

You can't tell me you ain't cryin', Black. You can't tell me you ain't missin' the ones that ain't neva comin' back.

You can't tell me you ain't cryin', Black. You can't tell me you ain't cried them hard tears, they can break yo' back.

You can't tell me city life ain't hard, you could be gone like that.

<u>Verse 1</u>

Black – shot dead in "The D", mad gory

not your kin? that don't change a sad story

they say "whose the realest one?" is the category

check Brightmoor, for sure, find me in the inventory

for all my victories, to Jah be the glory

if you don't believe then you prolly ain't for me

I'm a young one, with angels surrounding

no such thing as unconditional, only abounding

how you soundin'?

yall hit a lick on my block

we ain't call in no cops

but we strapped

we ain't resort to no violence

or install more sirens

tell y'all b****** came up with that

y'all ain't neva work for it

just dodged, ducked, robbed and cut for it

killed ma dude for the buffs on 'em

guess y'all tough

but it's that Black that you need

and not 'til you get shot will you see—

you know everybody bleeds

You can't tell me you ain't cryin', Black. You can't tell me you ain't missin' the ones that ain't neva comin' back.

You can't tell me you ain't cryin', Black. You can't tell me you ain't cried them hard tears, they can break yo' back.

You can't tell me you ain't cryin', Black. You can't tell me you ain't missin' the ones that ain't neva comin' back.

You can't tell me you ain't cryin', Black. You can't tell me city life ain't hard, you could be gone like that.

<u>Verse 2</u>

I ain't mad that you survivin'

really gotta kill the next man to keep thrivin'?

just unload yo ammo and keep drivin'

coward s***, cappin' kings 'fo they prime

and yes, these are the times

but I ain't wish for these

only six degrees and

that's in or out the streets

cappin' people daily

no time for hide and seek

save some time for me

there's so much I wanna be

try to dry the tears

and they just keep fallin'

count up all the years

dat ya mans keep callin'

got the phone line on

that's if nothing else

can't leave all this Black love

sittin' on the shelf

I know you know this well –

Can't tell me you ain't cryin' Black…

You can't tell me you ain't missin' the ones that ain't neva comin' back.

You can't tell me you ain't cryin', Black. You can't tell me you ain't cried them hard tears, they can break yo' back.

You can't tell me you ain't cryin', Black. You can't tell me you ain't missin' the ones that ain't neva comin' back.

You can't tell me city life ain't hard, you could be gone like that.

"Holier than thou"

And yet, still human every moment of every day.

Still human, when each day ends.

You are human.

Human, like the rest of us.

Holy?...

only relatively.

"First African American to…"

No…

just the first one

that they know about.

We did it ALL, first.

…Read that again.

Civil Rights Act of 2020

And our roles

will be what they are.

Already.

My role will be

what it has

always been.

To keep record.

To keep account.

I am never

MIA.

My Black People.

Never bleeding,

breaking,

blue…

by yourselves.

There's an uprising

inside me.

The strength of

ten trillion storms.

I am part

revolutionary

and part reserved.

I am part

redemptive

and part rebellious.

And part smoke.

I am not afraid,

to keep record.

Trust me,

to keep account.

My Black People.

of all the fires.

Not just

all the ashes

once all the evil

burns down.

What being American means

What it means to be American keeps changing for me. Not that I ever had much pride about America to begin with—and still. So, sometimes I feel ashamed… buried under all this unbelievable madness. At a total loss for words or explanation, more often than I'd like to admit. I am disturbed when thousands die, in droves, and we sit back and simply state "it is what it is". When you look around and end up wondering how you're even coping… how we can walk and talk after all the bricks thrown at us and on our life paths. What it means to be American keeps changing for me. Not that it was ever the best fit for me from the start. So, I find myself daring to change that…

Petals

Forget-Me-Nots

only when overcome by absolute passion, we pour into one another genuinely. we master the small things and commit to mastering all beyond as well. it's *that* passion inside us that births our ability to create, with someone else (our lover, for example) as muse. to do. to move with them truly at the forefront of your mind. whether it's baking their favorite or buying some *thing* they wished for. or being their safe space after a long, hard day and really being present and listening… it takes passion. to continue to show up, ready and willing and interested.

… to help them remember.

*Patrice Rushen – Forget-Me-Nots (1982)

Untitled (Airport Love)

Tinkered with time

and stole away

a weekend.

Got lost

and stayed there.

It was

how I saw

there was no one

but you,

waiting for that flight.

It was

how we never cared,

to check and see

if onlookers eventually

looked away.

It was

the woman,

enamored by

us fluttering our eyelashes

into one another's eyes.

It was how

all our arguments

got washed away

by our love's precipitate.

I want that back.

The bubble around us

that made

everything else fall away.

The way

our hands felt,

fingers interlaced.

The way my heart felt in your hands then, too.

The love we

constructed,

climbed inside of

and basked in

at the airport.

I sometimes wonder

if we misplaced

ourselves, mid-air…

if we could

free-fall back into love

somehow.

If we could

tinker

and steal away…

Disparate Elements

we are off balance

on a Tuesday.

where did all the love go?

did we destroy it

a month of Tuesdays ago?

we are procrastinating.

holding the love as our hostage,

until tomorrow comes.

and if it does not come,

I love you.

off balance. ragged. late on apologizing.

I still love you.

Good Grief (a failed relationship monologue)

After so many times, being hurt, the I love you's don't land in the pocket like they once did. The I love you's keep flying by, in fact, they never land. They never matter anymore. I know it's not your love for me that makes you act that way. So, I don't know what to call it any more since you say "it's not hate". Why is it so hard to admit that the trust is gone? What if there's something wrong that the other person can't fix; then what?... Will we always collapse?... Seems like so.

Up In Arms

the pain

inadvertent.

though

that does not soften the blows.

you made me beg you to be tender.

you pushed me

out of love with you.

then you would

try your best

to pull me back in.

My love never turns ugly.

Even when it's angry.

Even when it feels let down.

Your love…

you really act like

you don't know

how to love.

Like it's not in

your emotional capacity.

Loving you feels like

walking through

a field of land mines.

Like I need

a plan of attack.

And love should never

feel like that.

Shouldn't have me up in arms.

Karma

This is karma.

This is karma. This is not love.

That's why it comes, dressed like all love's made of.

So, you can get too far entangled

and lose your way.

Then feel the holes…

find your heart riddled with bullets

and realize that,

that was your price to pay.

Better Off

Better off without each other

Though it pains me to say

I think we really loved each other

Back in the day

And no, we aren't that old

But my feelings for you grew, years

I lay awake late at night sometimes

and I fight back tears

So sad to have to let you go

Cast you out of my heart

So sad the day I realized

We'd actually always been apart

I could no longer play the role

It got so hard to pretend

That you were truly good to me

That we were truly friends

You were never for me

I was sent to help you through

And that's why I'm okay now

Having a life with no more you

If I Needed You

I don't need you to notice me. You do that already. And I don't need you to let me in. You've done that in substantial ways. I only need you to be you. As that will mean there will always be space in you, for me. Or so I've told my heart to believe.

Broken One

I want to

un-love

you.

Take all of my love, back

from you.

We promised.

Nearly ten years ago now.

But you told our secret…

the one we said

we would never tell.

So much for your promise.

I would have

used all those ten years

to start un-loving you.

You are broken,

just like the promise you made.

Dramamine

I don't know that we exist beyond the time we just spent with one another.

I don't know that I want to, still, or am able to continue to be a friend to you.

It seems I've outgrown the me that could tolerate the way we speak to one another. I just can't do it anymore.

So tight-rope-tight.

Your communication style causes my mood to swing instantly?... Constantly?

You make me nauseous—

Learning to love you was such a bumpy ride.

I don't know if I ever really learned.

Seeds

A Note on Love #1,462

If there's a feeling greater than love, I wish someone would show it to me. point to it. spell it out for me directly. Because lately the love ain't—

The love has no weight on the dissipation of grief.

The love does not simplify the struggle.

The love does not quicken the heart to forgive any faster than it deems capable.

The love does not make the hard words easier to say.

If there's a feeling greater than love, I want to know it most intimately.

How to hold space when I feel like I have none left to situate.

How to stand tall and make sensical syntax out of my feelings.

How to deliver love, in all its fragility, with the right amount of pressure and from the right angles.

The love does not expect more from you, the person does.

And all this love can't reverse time.

All this love can't make you believe, remember or forget.

We all want someone who is down for us. Real love.

A love that truly knows what's best for you because they've studied you fervently.

A love that will break sleep for you. At whatever time, for you.

Roadside service, on-call, "I'mma be there when you break down" kind of love.

A love that never feels like work. Always feels like sabbatical…

The smell of you

I caught your scent in the air, but someone else was wearing it. The thought of you snatched my heart right out of my chest; in a snap! Before it got snatched, I felt deep pounds of it plump through my body, like a beating vibration, before my heart flew away into my thoughts and my tears. First, involuntary and pleasurable. Now, pain. Thinking of that time I just couldn't let you leave without kissing you first. We were there by the entryway, the door. I'd never felt a kiss so right and I haven't since. Not even from you again. Licks and sucks with perfect timing. We seamlessly made love with our mouths; moans sprinkled on top of the moments. You grabbed for me and I came closer, slave to your touch. Your body pressed against mine and mine pressed against the wall... I couldn't escape and I didn't want to. And we kissed. *I know you remember this.*

Feels So Right

Being with you

last night

felt like a supernatural spell.

Today is here

and I'm eager to know

every scheme up your sleeves.

Place Your Hands

The best

I can explain

is that

the whole world

feels different

when you're holding me.

Borders

You know that one thing

that happened

that you will

take to your grave?

Secrets;

no respect of person.

It's just

some s***

has to stay inside.

And you can't get full swallowing lies

Would you believe

I lied

so

elaborately

because that's how much

I loved you?

Too much

to hurt you

with my truths.

Confused Heart

I have to choose

whether to believe

your love professions,

amidst your harsh critiques.

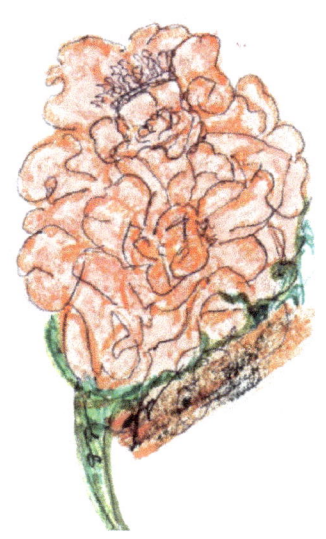

And so, you'll never get a taste…

Dropped some hot truth on your plate. But you're already too full of the wrong things to even consider taking a bite.

Thermal

I miss your body heat

and what it does to me.

Like a script

Rehearse you, like I'm an actress

Learn you, line by line

In and outside of parenthesis

Philodendron

Nowadays

During these uncertain and difficult times…

The Plague

This insomnia is spiritual.

There isn't enough space

in my heart.

for all my kind

to come inside and be safe.

immune or asymptomatic.

death looks the same to us all.

Quarantine

gifted me writing. And blocks… on other fronts. I am writing what I want but also, what flows most naturally for my every moment.

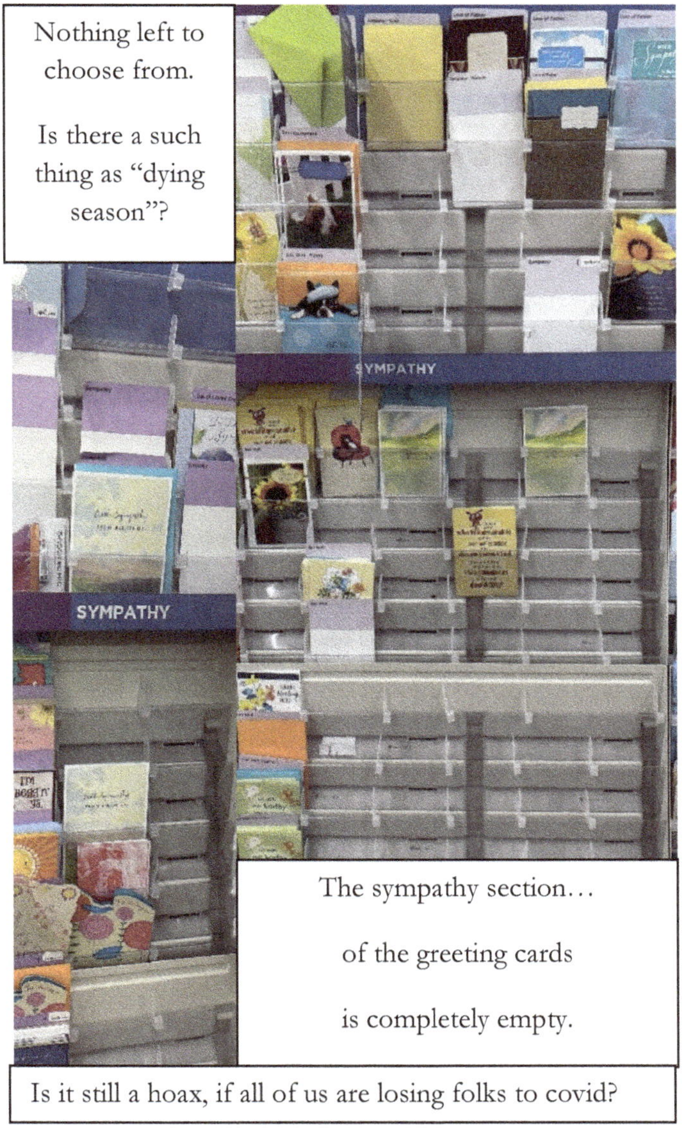

Nothing left to choose from.

Is there a such thing as "dying season"?

The sympathy section…

of the greeting cards

is completely empty.

Is it still a hoax, if all of us are losing folks to covid?

PANDEMIC

Partly confused. Partial. Participating.

Anxious. Agitated. Awake.

No. Not now. Never.

Disengaged. Damaged. Drained.

Exhausted. Essential. Expected.

Mind-altering. Managing. Mental.

Invasion. Ineligible. Insistent.

Concerned. Courageous. Captive.

Georgia Rain

Georgia is a place where a cloud will find you and rain on you. Just you. For as long as it wants. And then the sun comes back out… and it will find you too. Dry up all the rain.

P&DC

I used to be able to silence my discomfort by stuffing all of my feelings inside an APC. would push them to the dock and trust they would be shipped off, far away from me somehow. and when they came back, I tried packing them inside a BMC. thinking what I needed was more storage space for the monotony and slow death of my creative self. called myself packing them down tight. like they were going to take flight. and now accepting that no container of any size will do; with a better understanding of 'blue flu'; surprising myself as I'm smarter than I ever knew; a container is the last thing I need from the P&DC.

Racism is not a feeling

How do we know, as Black people, which smiling faces are for us or against us? We expect loyalty from strangers… and that might be fine if our safety was not a literal concern. This hatred has not been dormant for decades; it's been brewing and revamping and recycling itself through branches and limbs of family trees across the nation. Tell me these modern-day-lynchings and even strange fruit, still hanging… are not real… it seems we are unheard as Black people. The deaths tally up, even if they are never broadcasted on the daily. We have *been* here. We have *been* being treated unfairly. We have been being hunted, raped, tortured and ignored. And as a young, Black woman I am tired of s*** being unfair. The s*** is not a feeling; it's the reality I'm living.

Racism is not a feeling.

NOW

there's a

narcissist in me

overpowering the

whole of me

Sick

they say "trust the process"

or "let it run its course".

knowing damn well

we humans

are too afraid of the unknown

"to trust"…

Running out of it

Quite frankly, I'm breaking down

Unable to process it all

All around me, peace has vanished

Running in place, while lives are ruined

And can't find the antidote

No cure for all that's gone wrong

The ways I feel have formed a mountain

I need space from all that's closing in

Need time to mend the broken pieces

Even if they can't be mended and there will never be immunity. We just need more time and it feels like we're running out of it.

If Only… (a poem for Wilson Ali Calvin)

If I was told I could find you where the river opens up to the ocean, I promise I would swim in search of you, faster and faster, until my arms grew numb.

I would walk a million miles over summer-baked-sand if I thought the pier was where you would be. I would cross each wooden plank, with the sun's sting on my back and dock there and daydream with you.

If I was told right now that my loudest singing voice would bring you back for one more laugh, I promise I would go hoarse belting towards the sky with melody. Just for one more laugh.

I would chase after every rainbow and every sunset, if it meant you would be the pot of gold. We would sit in awe at the beauty of it all.

I would wait at the base of a cherry tree for hours on end if I knew that you would eventually come and sit down next to me. We would bite down and make a wish, before tossing the stems and pits.

If I was told that opening the throttle on a long wide road would leave me straight to you, I would gather my courage and speed until the destination that is you came into view.

If only I could have one more conversation with you, I promise I would remind you of how there's nothing I wouldn't do for you. And you would feel the strength of my love in that moment, as fiercely as I feel the weight of your absence right now.

Losing You

Wilson…

I think about the scream

your mother let out

when they closed your casket.

I cannot reach the place

within me that

I felt her pain in—

maybe the

same, unreachable space; past…

her heart and soul.

unspeakable.

your mother's scream

pierced blood and bone.

changed minds, hearts and bodies.

changed me.

It was the sound of losing you…

I've lived my life for so many other people

Before now

I feel like I let myself live for

so many other people.

The bullies who would just never let me be.

The friends I wanted to keep.

The parents I did not want to disappoint.

The lovers…

to save them from discomfort, tears, the real me.

The fear inside me that I let feel like a separate and powerful, living person inside me.

The pastors, paid in tithes to convict my soul and keep my spirit in line.

The saints and their steady stares.

The weird questions, the unfair and unfitting assumptions.

The elders who are wise, with their hurtful words and traditions.

The children, classmates, teammates, peers and coworkers that I just never quite fit into—

…

Now I just simply live my life for me.

Meet the Artists

Gwendolyn "G.G. Bank$" Apacanis, 81, is a multifaceted artist and painter who resides in Detroit, Michigan. She loves going shopping for stationary, trying new foods and making and giving gifts. Apacanis is inspired by themes of God and spirituality as well as animals and nature. She works across several mediums (i.e. stippling and free hand sketch, charcoal, acrylic, pastel) and loves to live-sketch people and places. She is most grateful for her family, her church and creative communities, and for art in all its facets.

Zellia Enjoli Tatiana (B.K.A. "Zee") is a master of free-verse poetry, dynamic storyteller and an independent artist. Born and raised in Detroit, Michigan, she loves sneakers and cool socks and collecting stickers and sleek, toy cars. The writer in Zee is inspired by illustrating truth and beauty as the perfect affinity. She writes fearlessly about love between women and the intersections of her own identity and life. "Flowers, only if they're from you" is her fifth self-published release, in collaboration with her grandmother, artist G.G. Bank$.

www.zelliaenjoli.com

Instagram	@inifinizeeandbeyond
FanBase	@ infinizeeandbeyond
YouTube	@infinizeeandbeyond
TikTok	@infinizeeandbeyond

Coming Next from Zellia Enjoli Tatiana

Just In Case the World Ends (a novel)

As an artist, you will be tasked with new work, new ideas. It's up to you to bring them from your imagination into real-life. You either make them become, or it seems like they are dormant inside you. You may forget or repress these ideas. I have been learning not to run from that initial feeling; it's almost like anxiety. It's actually a good sign. Your heart racing means greatness is upon you and triumph is closer than it's ever been. I get that feeling sometimes when I sit down to write. I have also been learning to stop in my tracks and show reverence to the creative voice inside me. To not trust myself to remember it later on because I won't. Then I'll end up begging God to send it back around to me one more time. Just stop and write it down or sketch it out.

Your favorite song started out as a token thought, or half a melody of a hum. The artist made it fully become what they felt it should be. Your favorite restaurant may be the fruit of a man's wish and hard work. He had to manifest, before you could have an unprecedented, fine dining experience though. All art has a moment of initial conception... that we then grow and translate into a moment of birth.

I love how I know exactly what I mean; and the art aspect of writing free verse poetry means that my words will always mean something different to someone else. Always. Maybe much different than what I intended to convey. Some artists see this as frustrating and I view it as all-powerful.

Transcendental. I love how poetry doesn't have to be chronological. It doesn't have to be read in sequence or all at once. I love how poems are like moments for me. Sometimes merely memories of moments.

Keep creating. It's always, all worth it.

Love,

Zee